THIRTY

LIFE LESSONS I LEARNT IN MY JOURNEY TILL

THIRTY

A self care journal by a millennial

Dr. Shefali Singh, PhD

You matter...

your perspective matters..

your satisfaction matters..

and most importantly..

it's **"your happiness"** that matters..

Just make it happen!

Dear you,

"Thirty life lessons I learnt in my journey till Thirty" AKA 30 by 30 was the idea that came to my mind when I was calculating my age a month before my 31st birthday. I've experienced numerous events in my life and witnessed changes in my surroundings, each offering valuable lessons. Determined to preserve these experiences and lessons, I've decided to make them truly unforgettable.

Life has taught me so many lessons; both good and challenging. Believe me, they all are the reason or rather result of what I am today and I am proud of myself.

No matter how emotional I can be sometimes but what I love in me is I am confident, satisfied & happy and that's what matters… matters the most…

This book is short, crisp and contains thirty lessons or I can say learnings of my journey till 30 years of age.

Go slow with this book. Try to implement these lessons in your daily life and see the magic of satisfaction and happiness within yourself.

From

Me….

THANK YOU !

My motivation and my strength , my husband.

My parents and family members for their never ending support.

The baby in my tummy who is just busy kicking and punching while I am writing this.

Thank you my three angels for giving the truthful feedback on the first draft and making it happen.

And thank you to all the people who are involved directly or indirectly in teaching me these lessons.

The very first question

Is this Book Suitable for Readers Below or Above 30 Years of Age?

Absolutely!

This book covers everyday habits that can be adopted at any stage of life, whether you're 3, 30, or 60 years old.

CHAPTERS

Let's skip giving titles and numbers to these life lessons.

Take it easy, read them randomly, whenever and wherever you like, in

your own way.

1.
2.
3.
4.
5.
6.
7.
8.
9.
10.
11.
12.
13.
14.
15.
16.
17.
18.
19.
20.
21.
22.
23.
24.
25.
26.
27.
28.
29.
30.

Remember to have a pen handy every time to read this book.

The Power of Gratefulness

Gratefulness is a wondrous state of mind that allows us to appreciate the goodness and blessings in our lives. It is a simple yet profound emotion that opens the door to happiness, contentment, and inner peace. When we cultivate a grateful heart, we shift our focus from what we lack to what we already have, transforming our perspective and enriching our daily experiences.

Gratefulness is an art of finding joy in the little things, acknowledging the people who bring love and support, and cherishing the moments that make life extraordinary.

Benefits of practicing gratitude

Practicing gratitude has far-reaching benefits that extend to our mental, emotional, and physical well-being. Gratefulness nurtures positive emotions and reduces feelings of anxiety and depression. Expressing gratitude strengthens bonds with others and fosters a sense of connection. Grateful individuals are better equipped to navigate life's challenges with resilience and optimism.

A grateful mind finds it easier to relax and enjoy restful sleep. It encourages us to recognize and appreciate the kindness and generosity of others and hen we acknowledge our blessings, we cultivate a positive self-image and greater self-acceptance.

Bringing Gratefulness into Your Life

- Gratitude Journal: Write down three things you are grateful for. Reflect on the positive aspects of your day and the blessings you have received.

1.

2.

3.

- Show gratitude: Give a hug to someone who is sad, to someone who is upset, someone who is happy or the one who is working hard for the whole day. Acknowledge and appreciate, surprise and encourage them.
- Help someone: Be it your neighbor, member of your family, or a stranger. Just help and make them feel happy. Compliment others for things they do, food they cook, or efforts they make.
- Thank-You Notes: Express your gratitude to friends, family, and colleagues through handwritten thank-you notes. Simple gestures of appreciation can brighten someone's day. Remember your handwritten "thank you" can make a big difference in their life.

Tried And Tested. Give It A Try!

- Gratitude Walk: Once in a while, take a leisurely walk in nature and focus on the beauty around you. Be thankful for the sights, sounds, and sensations that nature offers.
- Morning Gratitude: We get busy in our day to day work so much that we usually forget to see beautiful things around and cherish them.

> "Be thankful for the food you eat, place you live, family that matters
> and life you have"

Research shows that practicing gratitude leads to improved mental well-being and happiness. In a study by Emmons and McCullough (2003), participants who kept a gratitude journal reported feeling more optimistic and satisfied with their lives. Additionally, Wood, Froh, and Geraghty (2010) found that gratitude is associated with better physical health, improved relationships, and enhanced sleep quality.

Embrace the magic of gratefulness, and you will discover that a life filled with appreciation and thankfulness is a life overflowing with happiness and fulfillment.

1. Emmons, R. A., & McCullough, M. E. (2003). Counting blessings versus burdens: An experimental investigation of gratitude and subjective well-being in daily life. Journal of Personality and Social Psychology, 84(2), 377–389. [DOI: 10.1037/0022-3514.84.2.377]

2. Wood, A. M., Froh, J. J., & Geraghty, A. W. A. (2010). Gratitude and well-being: A review and theoretical integration. Clinical Psychology Review, 30(7), 890–905. [DOI: 10.1016/j.cpr.2010.03.005]

Gratitude Galore

	Five Things/People In My Life, I Am Thankful
1.	
2.	
3.	
4.	
5.	

Pick out at least one person (you can select more) you are thankful to.

Write a note/message/card to that person expressing your "Thank You" to them.

A Smile: The Sunshine Within

A smile, the universal language of happiness, is a simple yet incredibly powerful expression. It's a beautiful curve that sets everything straight, a silent communicator of joy, kindness, and warmth. A smile is the reflection of your inner sunshine, a gift you can share with others every day.

Think of the smell of the first rain..The plate of your favorite food.
Smile is that feeling and expression which makes your moment happy and content.
It is the expression of showing love and happiness.

In a world filled with hustle and bustle, we often underestimate the enchanting magic that a smile can bring.

Incorporating more smiles into your daily life can significantly boost your well-being and relationships. Smiling triggers the release of endorphins, reducing stress and improving mood. It fosters connections by signaling friendliness and approachability, enhancing likeability and trustworthiness.

Moreover, smiling boosts confidence and self-esteem, aiding in tackling challenges and seizing opportunities. It may also contribute to better physical health, including a strengthened immune system and potential benefits for heart health. In conflicts, smiling can ease tensions and promote resolution by fostering empathy and understanding.

Being friendly at work can help you work better with others and move up in your career. Plus, smiling often can help you feel happier and deal with tough times better. Incorporating more smiles into your daily interactions is a simple yet powerful way to enhance well-being and cultivate positive relationships, benefiting both yourself and those around you.

- Smile Mirror: Make it a habit to smile at yourself in the mirror every morning. It sets a positive tone for your day and reminds you to carry that smile with you.
- Random Acts of Kindness: Challenge yourself to perform small acts of kindness throughout the day. Holding the door for someone, helping others around, or complimenting a stranger can all be accompanied by a genuine smile.
- Smile Meditation: Practice smile meditation, where you sit in a quiet place, close your eyes, and focus on the sensation of smiling. Let this feeling of warmth and joy permeate your entire being.

Remember, your smile is your superpower. It brightens your life and the lives of those you encounter. So, wear it proudly and share it generously.

DO YOU KNOW?

Ever noticed how a smile can spread like a happy wave in a group?

It's called the **Ripple Effect.** It's like passing around good vibes – one person smiles, and suddenly everyone's feeling a bit brighter. Emotional contagion, they call it. A shared smile creates a chain reaction, spreading joy and positivity. It's a sweet reminder that our emotions are connected, and a simple smile can create a feel-good domino effect in a group.

Let's try it //

While I was editing the first draft of this book, my one-year-old came up to me and kissed my hand, sweetly saying, "MUMMA"....

It melted my heart and brought the most satisfying smile to my face.

Close your eyes and think of the one thing that made you smile today.

Wait! If you're having a "not so good" day, get up and do something that makes you happy. Call a friend, listen to music, cook your favorite dish, or simply go out and indulge in your favorite street food.

The only thing that matters is your Smile.

The Essence of Help: Power of Assistance

Help, simply put, is extending a hand, lending an ear, or offering support when someone needs it. It's the act of being there for others, selflessly and compassionately.

In a world that sometimes seems self-centered and fast-paced, the concept of help is like a soothing **balm for the soul**. It's an essential element in building stronger relationships, fostering a sense of community, and making the world a better place.

As the saying goes, "No act of kindness, no matter how small, is ever wasted." - Aesop

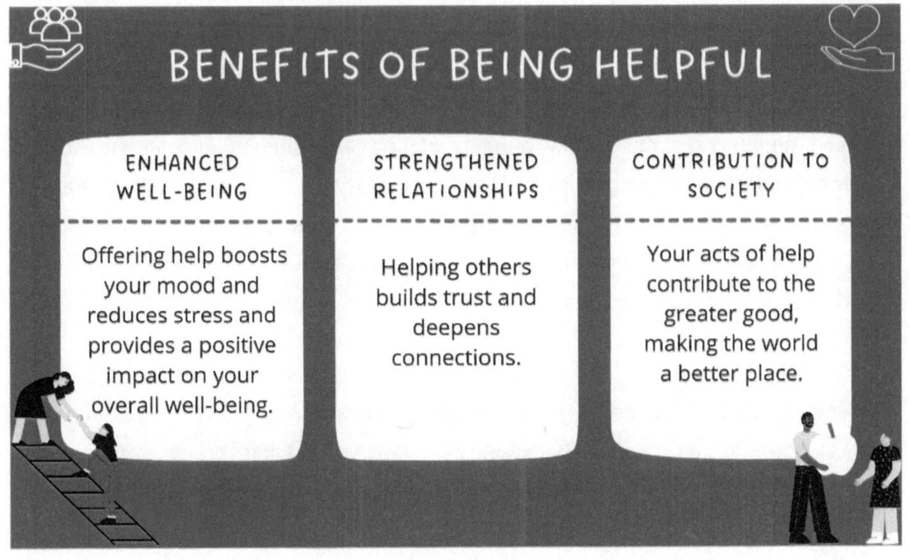

- Start Small: Help doesn't have to be grand gestures. Hold the door for someone, offer your seat, or even smile at a stranger.
- Listen Actively: Sometimes, all someone needs is a listening ear. Pay attention to others, ask questions, and show genuine interest in their stories.
- Volunteer: Donate your time. Volunteering is a fantastic way to give back to your community. Offer your skills or knowledge to someone who might benefit from them. We all have something to share.
- Random Acts of Kindness: Dedicate a part of your day to perform random acts of kindness. It could be as simple as helping someone around you ne it home, office or neighborhood.

A study conducted by researchers at the University of California, Berkeley, and Harvard Business School found that acts of kindness and assistance don't just benefit the recipient; they also have significant positive effects on the giver's well-being (Aknin et al., 2013). The study, published in the journal Psychological Science, showed that individuals who regularly engaged in acts of kindness and assistance towards others experienced increased levels of **happiness, satisfaction, and overall well-being.** This research underscores the mutual benefits of help and support in fostering positive emotions and strengthening social connections. So, by extending a helping hand to others, not only are you making a difference in their lives, but you're also enhancing your own happiness and fulfillment. It's a win-win situation that highlights the profound impact of simple acts of kindness on our well-being.

Remember, help isn't just about giving; it's also about receiving. Don't hesitate to ask for assistance when you need it. By fostering a culture of help and support, we create a world where compassion and empathy thrive, making life more beautiful for everyone.

Aknin, L. B., Broesch, T., Hamlin, J. K., & Van de Vondervoort, J. W. (2013). Prosocial behavior leads to happiness in a small-scale rural society. Psychological Science, 24(6), 1-9.

Helping hand..

Observe your surroundings and find opportunities to lend a hand.

Take a few minutes to assist others in any way you can. Here are some ideas:

- ○ Offer assistance with daily tasks.
- ○ Extend help in cooking or preparing meals.
- ○ Support in cleaning and organizing shared spaces.
- ○ Provide a helping hand in running errands.
- ○ Be available for someone who needs a listening ear.
- ○ Help with gardening or outdoor tasks.
- ○ Assist with technology or computer-related issues.

What are you planning to do?____

Hope - A Beacon of Light

In the darkest of times, hope is the light that guides us towards a brighter tomorrow. It is an emotion that uplifts the spirit, and a force that propels us forward.

Hope is more than just a wish or a desire; it's the belief that something positive can happen despite the odds. It's the unwavering faith that even when life throws challenges our way, there's a possibility for a better outcome.

Hope is the fuel that keeps our dreams alive and our hearts resilient. Hope acts as a natural stress reducer. When you believe that better days are ahead, your body responds by releasing fewer stress hormones, keeping anxiety at bay.

- Improved Health: Studies have shown that hopeful individuals tend to have stronger immune systems and faster recovery rates from illness. Hope is a powerful medicine for the body.
- Enhanced Creativity: Hope inspires creativity. When you're hopeful, your mind is open to new possibilities, and you're more likely to find innovative solutions to problems.

Nurturing Hope in Your Life

- Set Realistic Goals: Break your long-term goals into smaller, achievable steps. Each step accomplished fuels your hope and motivation.
- Surround Yourself with Positivity: Spend time with people who uplift you and share your dreams. Positive social connections can boost your hope.
- Practice Gratitude: Reflect on the things you're grateful for daily. It shifts your focus from what's lacking to what's abundant in your life.
- Learn and Grow: Invest time in learning new skills or pursuing hobbies. The sense of accomplishment from mastering something new can boost hope.
- Mindful Breathing: Practice deep breathing exercises to stay present and calm. A calm mind is more open to hope.

Hope is a precious gift you can give to yourself, and it costs nothing. Embrace hope, nurture it, and let it guide you on your journey toward a brighter, more fulfilling life.

I have a small black board in front of my work desk. I always write down my tasks and goals there and strike them when done.

Looking at your own progress keeps you going and motivated.

Try writing down your hopes, dreams, and what you've achieved.

Put it near your work area or bed and mark off your progress.

Seeing your goals on paper can really boost your motivation.

Discovering your Breathe

Have you ever stopped to truly appreciate the simple act of breathing? Breath is the rhythmic inhalation and exhalation of air, essential for sustaining life. It's something we do unconsciously, yet its impact on our physical and mental well-being is profound.

The Breath's Secret: As author Anais Nin once wisely said, "Life shrinks or expands in proportion to one's courage." Similarly, the power of breath expands in proportion to our awareness of it. When we pause to breathe consciously, we tap into a wellspring of vitality and inner strength that lies within us.

We all know that breathing is a continuous and natural process. Our body breathes naturally but here I'm referring to breathing "***intentionally***".

If you are feeling tired, breathe deeply, if you are anxious ... breathe deeply...to breathe means to focus on your inhaling and exhaling...especially by closing your eyes and focusing on your breath.

Close your eyes and inhale and exhale deeply three times..........
1.....................
2.....................
3.....................

How do you feel?
Relaxed?
Calm?

- Conscious breathing activates the body's relaxation response, reducing stress levels and promoting a sense of calm.
- A few deep breaths can sharpen your concentration and improve your decision-making abilities.
- Deep and deliberate breathing can boost your immune system and aid in digestion, benefiting your overall well-being.

Incorporating Mindful Breathing into your daily routine

- Morning Ritual: Start your day with a few minutes of deep, intentional breathing. Just inhale and exhale.
- Breath Breaks: Throughout your day, take short breaks to practice deep breathing. Even a minute of conscious breath can rejuvenate your mind and body.
- Bedtime Relaxation: Before sleep, engage in a relaxing breathing exercise to release tension and prepare your mind for restful slumber.
- Breath-Centric Yoga: Focus on conscious breathing during your yoga routine, matching each breath to your poses for a stronger mind-body connection.

By practicing conscious breathing and integrating it into our daily routines, we can unlock a profound source of well-being, resilience, and peace. Embrace the power of your breath, and you'll discover a path to a more vibrant and harmonious life.

CONSCIOUS BREATHING

Conscious breathing is the intentional and mindful act of paying attention to one's breath, often with the purpose of promoting relaxation, reducing stress, or enhancing overall well-being.

It involves being aware of each inhalation and exhalation, focusing on the rhythm and depth of breath, and using breathing techniques to bring about a sense of calm and presence in the current moment.

Conscious breathing is a common element in practices such as meditation, mindfulness, and certain relaxation exercises.

Sit in a comfortable position, Make sure you are sitting in a space free from noises.
Close your eyes and take 10 deep breaths.
Just observe the deep inhales and exhales and nothing else.

Pen down how you feel

....
....
....
....

If it was relaxing, make it a daily habit.

Tip- You can set a daily reminder in your phone.

The Art of Self-Pampering

Pampering is a delightful act of self-love and self-care. It involves treating yourself with kindness and affection, allowing you to recharge, relax, and rejuvenate. It's a way of acknowledging your worth and nurturing your well-being.

Imagine this: You've had a long, tiring day, and you finally find a moment to unwind. Instead of reaching for your phone or diving into work, you decide to pamper yourself. Play your favorite music, sit on a comfortable corner, and sip our favorite drink As you soak in this simple pleasure, you can feel your stress melting away, leaving you refreshed and content.

"Self-care is not selfish. You cannot serve from an empty vessel." -Eleanor Brownn

- Pampering provides an oasis of calm in your busy life, helping to reduce stress levels and promote relaxation.
- Taking time for yourself can boost your mood and improve your overall mental well-being.
- Pampering reinforces your self-worth, reminding you that you deserve to be treated with care and kindness.
- Relaxation and self-care can have a positive impact on your physical health, including better sleep and reduced muscle tension.

How can you pamper yourself without adding too much effort, time and energy?

- Indulge in Your Favorite Beverage: Whether it's a cup of coffee, tea, or a smoothie, take time to savor your favorite drink without distractions like the phone or TV. This is a simple way to pamper yourself and enjoy the moment.

- Unplug: Dedicate some time each day to disconnect from screens and technology. Use this time to read a book, journal, or simply sit in silence, providing a pampering break for your mind away from the constant buzz of digital life.
- Nature Walks: Spend a few minutes in nature every day, whether it's a walk in the park or just sitting in your garden. Connect with the natural world around you, allowing the soothing environment to pamper your senses and promote relaxation.
- DIY Spa: Once a week, indulge in a mini spa night at home. Use facial masks, exfoliate, and pamper your skin. Regardless of gender, dedicating time to pamper and care for your skin is a self-care ritual that can leave you feeling refreshed and revitalized.
- Read a Good Book: Reading is a wonderful way to escape into a different world and pamper your mind. Choose a book that captivates your imagination.
- Practice Mindfulness: Engage in meditation or mindfulness exercises. This helps you connect with your inner self and reduces stress.
- Cook a Meal: Try your hand at cooking a special meal or order your favorite dish from a restaurant. Enjoying delicious food is a delightful form of self-pampering.
- Explore Art and Creativity: Engaging in creative activities such as painting, drawing, or crafting can be incredibly fulfilling.
- Enjoy Music: Put on your favorite music. Music has the power to uplift your mood.

When was the last time you treated yourself to something that brought genuine happiness and comfort?

The art of pampering goes beyond mere indulgence; it involves giving special attention to your well-being.

- Take a moment to prioritize yourself and relish in the joy it brings. Whether it's indulging in a long overdue hobby, in a hot/cold bath, or enjoying spa treatments, these acts not only ease muscle tension and enhance flexibility but also reduce stress hormone activity, improve concentration, and boost overall mood.

- Engaging in self-care rituals contributes to improved bodily functions, including blood flow and digestion, while increasing both physical and mental energy. From managing chronic pain to enhancing skin clarity, the benefits are manifold. So, light a fragrant candle, play soothing music, or wear your favorite piece of jewelry as you engage in activities that bring you joy. Consider this a gentle reminder: pampering yourself is not just a luxury, but a necessity for your confidence, happiness, and overall well-being.

And don't forget, spreading this care to your loved ones can create a ripple effect of positivity.

Psychological priming

Psychological priming refers to the phenomenon where exposure to one stimulus influences a person's response to a subsequent stimulus. Essentially, it's the idea that our perception and reaction to something can be influenced by our prior experiences or exposure to related stimuli. This can happen consciously or unconsciously and can affect various aspects of cognition, emotion, and behavior.

For example, if someone regularly associates the scent of lavender with relaxation because they use lavender-scented products during self-care routines, the smell of lavender may prime their brain to feel more relaxed when they encounter it again in the future. This priming effect can enhance the enjoyment and benefits of pampering activities.

The priming effect can also influence the purchasing decisions and overall perception of the product.

If a person regularly sees commercials associating a particular brand of coffee with feelings of comfort and relaxation, they may be primed to feel more positively about that brand when they encounter it in a store, even if they're not consciously aware of the influence of the commercials.

Discover Your Happy Haven

Think of one thing which makes you feel relaxed and happy at the same time.

Is it sleeping? Or listening to music?

For some, it can be dancing while for others it can be going to a salon. Be it meditation, outdoor activity, getting dressed, shopping, exercising or doing nothing; think of that one thing which makes you feel pampered.

- What is the one thing which makes you happy and pampered?

- Give yourself sometime and indulge yourself in that activity/thing.

- Pen down how you feel..

....

....

....

....

Incorporate simple pampering practices into your routine, and you'll find that these small acts make a significant difference. Cultivate the habit of giving yourself a break and treating yourself positively. This not only brings happiness but also enhances your overall productivity.

Engaging with Purpose and Passion

Engagement is like the spark that sets your life on fire. It's the art of immersing yourself fully in the present moment, connecting with your inner passions, and experiencing life with a sense of purpose and enthusiasm. When you engage, you don't just go through the motions; you savor every moment, making the most of your time on this beautiful journey called *life*.

Engaging with life offers a myriad of benefits. It leads to increased happiness, reduced stress, and improved overall well-being. When you're fully engaged, you become more creative, more productive, and better at problem-solving. Here are some practical ideas to keep you engaged with purpose and passion-

- Mindful Moments: Engage yourself with a few minutes of simple mindfulness. Focus on your breath and the sensations in your body. This simple practice can ground you in the present moment and set a positive tone for the day.
- Discover Passions: Make a list of activities or hobbies that truly excite you. Whether it's painting, dancing, hiking, or cooking, set aside time each week/month to pursue these passions.
- Connect with Others: Engage with friends and loved ones by truly listening when they speak. Show genuine interest in their lives, and you'll find your relationships grow stronger.
- Limit Distractions: In a world filled with digital distractions, take breaks from screens and enjoy the real world around you. Go for a walk, read a book, or simply sit in silence and observe the world.
- Unplug Time: Set aside at least 30 minutes each day to disconnect from your devices. Use this time to engage with a hobby or spend quality time with loved ones.
- Nature Connection: Spend time outdoors. Whether it's a short walk in the park or a weekend hike, nature has a way of grounding us and fostering a deep sense of engagement.

Remember, engagement is not a destination; it's a lifelong journey. It is all about active involvement, taking a moment each day to do something meaningful for yourself.
In the midst of your busy schedule, allocate time for an activity that resonates with your passions, keeping in mind the key principles of staying "healthy and happy."

While various activities can bring joy, the focus here is on those that contribute positively to your well-being. Whether it's pursuing a hobby like cooking, dancing, or writing, connecting with loved ones, furthering your education through online certifications, playing sports, reading, or creating personal challenges, each endeavor plays a role in making you healthier, happier, and more fulfilled. By engaging in these activities, you not only reduce stress but also enhance your productivity, build confidence, and elevate emotional intelligence.

Take a moment to reflect on your feelings, set goals, and stimulate creativity. In the process, you become the reason for your own smile, fostering a balanced and content life. So, embrace the concept of engagement—whether it's through exercise, learning, socializing, or self-care—and let it be a daily ritual that enriches your life on various levels. Remember, it's not just about what you are doing; it's about the act of doing itself.

Let's keep you busy

Every day, I immerse myself in the activities of cooking and writing, both of which are my true passions, bringing me immense satisfaction.

What activities engage you, bringing both happiness and motivation simultaneously? Reflect on the things that truly captivate your interest and spark joy in your life. Now, challenge yourself to actively engage in one of these activities into your routine at least once a week.

____

____

____

____

By deliberately engaging in activities aligned with your passions, you not only cultivate a sense of fulfillment but also contribute to your overall well-being.
Let's embark on this journey of self-discovery and intentional engagement to enhance the quality of our lives.

Unleash Your Creative Mastery

Creativity is like a treasure hidden within you, waiting to be discovered. It's the ability to generate original ideas, solutions, or expressions through imaginative thinking. Creativity isn't just limited to artists and writers; it's a skill that can be nurtured and harnessed by anyone.

Being creative is like a breath of fresh air for your mind. It helps you learn better by letting you think in different ways, breaking old habits, and making you more curious.
Creativity is not just about you; it brings people together, helps you work as a team, and connects you with different cultures. It also boosts your confidence, making you less influenced by others.
So, whether you're drawing, asking questions, or solving problems, let your creativity shine – it's not just fun and joyful, but it also keeps your mind active and helps everyone learn in their own special way.

- Keep a diary and write down your thoughts, ideas, and dreams regularly. It's a great way to unleash your inner creativity and gain clarity.
- Surround Yourself with Inspiration- Decorate your workspace or home with things that inspire you, such as art, quotes, or nature elements.
- Try Something New- Explore a hobby or skill you've never tried before, like painting, playing a musical instrument, or cooking exotic dishes.
- Brainstorming Sessions- Collaborate with friends or colleagues for brainstorming sessions where you come up with new ideas and solutions together.

Have you ever engaged in Sudoku or tackled a crossword from the newspaper?

Challenge your mind with puzzles, riddles, or brain teasers to enhance critical and creative thinking skills.

Creativity is not just a talent; it's a mindset. It's about embracing the endless possibilities that lie within you and daring to explore them. So, let your creativity soar, and watch how it transforms your life into a masterpiece of innovation and inspiration.

Creativity is about turning your ideas into real things, and it's not just for art – you can be creative at work, in your kitchen, or while playing. The key is to do things in your unique and interesting way, without worrying about results. "Create everything you imagine" is a reminder to let your creativity flow without limits.

Divergent thinking

Divergent thinking is the engine that drives creativity, igniting the imagination to explore uncharted territories and envision new possibilities. When we engage in creative activities like brainstorming, we tap into the boundless realm of divergent thinking, where multiple pathways and solutions unfurl before us. By encouraging divergent thinking, we invite innovation to flourish, paving the way for fresh perspectives, unconventional ideas, and breakthrough creations. It's through this process of divergent thinking that the seeds of creativity are sown, ultimately blossoming into unique and transformative outcomes.

Creative Escapes

Ignite your creativity with a Doodle Fusion Challenge!

1. Start with a simple shape, like a circle or square, in the center of your paper.
2. Then, let your imagination run wild as you gradually transform that shape into a unique and intricate doodle.
3. Experiment with patterns, textures, and details, and allow one doodle element to seamlessly flow into the next.

The goal is to create a visually captivating and harmonious doodle that emerges organically. Not only does this activity engage your artistic flair, but it also encourages free-flowing creativity as you watch your doodle evolve into a masterpiece!

The Joy of Lifelong Learning

Learning is not just a word; it's a gateway to a world full of opportunities, growth, and self-discovery. It is more than just acquiring facts; it's a transformative experience that enriches your mind, broadens your horizons. It's a lifelong adventure that keeps your brain sharp and your spirit young.

The benefits of learning are boundless, from enhancing your problem-solving skills to boosting your self-esteem.

- Learning helps you discover your strengths and weaknesses, fostering a sense of self-awareness that guides your life choices.
- Continuous learning keeps your skills up-to-date, making you more valuable in the job market and opening doors to new career opportunities.
- Knowledge fosters better communication and understanding. When you learn about different cultures and perspectives, you can connect with people on a deeper level.
- Learning exposes you to new ideas, sparking creativity and innovation.

Everyday Learning Hacks:

1. Read daily to expand your mind.
2. Travel to gain new perspectives.
3. Take courses to boost your skills.
4. Learn from each other's experiences.

In essence, starting a learning journal and embracing the practice of learning from mistakes are not merely tasks; they are gateways to a lifelong journey of discovery and personal growth. The daily act of jotting down new insights, whether a word, a historical fact, or a fascinating concept, becomes a small yet impactful step in this journey.

Moreover, the invaluable lesson of learning from mistakes, analyzing missteps, making adjustments, and evolving from experiences transforms challenges into opportunities for development.

Remember, learning is a continuous expedition, not a final destination. With each passing day, you are presented with fresh chances to broaden your horizons. Approach these opportunities with curiosity and enthusiasm, for the joy of lifelong learning not only enriches the mind but also adds depth and vibrancy to life.

Let the pursuit of knowledge be your constant companion on this adventure, guiding you toward a brighter and more fulfilling future. Embrace the journey, savor the discoveries, and relish the transformative power of continuous learning.

Be open to learn

Today, while checking social media, I found an easy way to bake bread.
On my walk, I saw a mom and her daughter doing push-ups together.

What I learned: trying the new bread method and doing push-ups with my daughter.

Now, think about your day—what's the one thing you learned or noticed? Write it down
and give it a try soon.

Simplify Your Life: Unlocking the Power of Organization

Organization is the art of arranging and structuring things systematically, making it easier to find what you need when you need it. Organizing your life doesn't just save time; it also reduces stress, boosts productivity, and enhances your overall well-being.

Benefits of Organization:

- Reduced Stress: When you organize, you create a calming environment that reduces stress and promotes mental clarity.
- Increased Productivity: An organized workspace allows you to work more efficiently. You waste less time searching for things and can focus on what truly matters.
- Enhanced Creativity: A clutter-free mind fosters creativity. When your physical space is organized, your thoughts flow more freely.

Being organized isn't just about neatness; it's a lifestyle choice that can impact your well-being in profound ways, even potentially extending your lifespan. Research suggests that individuals who maintain an organized approach to life often adopt healthier habits, such as regular exercise and nutritious eating [Saxbe]. When your environment is clutter-free and your schedule is well-managed, you're more likely to prioritize self-care and make time for activities that promote physical and mental health. This commitment to organization not only fosters a sense of control and efficiency but also sets the stage for a longer and more fulfilling life. By proactively managing your time, space, and priorities, you're investing in your overall health and longevity, creating a foundation for wellness that can pay dividends well into the future.

Organization is a powerful tool that can simplify your life and unlock your full potential. As you embark on this journey to a more organized life, remember that it's not about perfection; it's about progress. With small, consistent efforts, you can experience the magic of organization and create a life filled with more time, less stress, and greater productivity.

Saxbe, D. E., Repetti, R. L., & Nishina, A. (2008). Marital satisfaction, recovery from work, and diurnal cortisol among men and women. Health Psychology, 27(1), 15–25. https://doi.org/10.1037/0278-6133.27.1.15

10-Tidy Minutes

1. Set a timer for 10 minutes.

2. Choose a small area in your home or workspace that needs tidying up. It could be your desk, a drawer, or a shelf.

3. Spend the 10 minutes cleaning and organizing that area. Put away items where they belong, throw away any trash, and straighten up the space.

Repeat this activity every day, focusing on a different area each time. Notice how even just 10 minutes of tidying up each day can make a big difference in keeping your space clean and organized over time.

(This is my favorite)

An Active Lifestyle for a Healthier and Happier Life

Being active is not just about hitting the gym or running marathons; it's a way of life that can lead to a healthier and happier you. Being active means engaging in physical activities that get your body moving and your heart pumping. It can be as simple as taking a brisk walk, dancing to your favorite music, or playing with your kids in the park. **The key is to keep your body in motion regularly.**

Here are some of the incredible benefits of an active lifestyle:

1. Improved Physical Health: Regular physical activity helps maintain a healthy weight, reduces the risk of chronic diseases like heart disease and diabetes, and boosts your immune system.
2. Enhanced Mental Well-being: Exercise releases endorphins, which can reduce stress and anxiety while improving your mood and overall mental health.
3. Increased Energy Levels: Staying active can give you more energy to tackle daily tasks and enjoy life to the fullest.
4. Better Sleep: Regular activity can promote better sleep patterns, ensuring you wake up feeling refreshed and rejuvenated.

Incorporating physical activity into your daily life doesn't have to be a daunting task. Start small, stay consistent, and remember that every little bit counts towards a healthier, happier you.

Staying healthy and active is the need of the hour.
Get up and do something for yourself.

What are you doing today? ....

Quality Over Quantity

In a world driven by numbers and metrics, it's easy to get caught up in the race for more—more likes, more possessions, more hours in the day. But what if I told you that the secret to a truly fulfilling life lies not in the quantity of things you have, but in the quality of those things?

"Quality over quantity" is a simple yet profound principle that emphasizes the importance of focusing on the value and excellence of what you have or do, rather than the sheer quantity or volume. It's about making deliberate choices and prioritizing the things, experiences, and relationships that truly matter to you.

- Evaluate Your Possessions: Declutter your living space by identifying items that hold true value and meaning to you. Donate or sell the rest.
- Prioritize quality time over quantity. Spend focused, undistracted moments with loved ones rather than constantly multitasking.
- In your professional life, commit to projects that align with your passions and skills, aiming for excellence rather than taking on too many responsibilities.
- Before making a purchase, ask yourself if it adds value to your life. Invest in high-quality items that last longer.
- Reflect on your day and identify moments of quality—meaningful conversations, satisfying achievements, or moments of genuine happiness.
- Read a book or article mindfully, absorbing the wisdom and knowledge it offers, rather than rushing through it.

Incorporating the principle of quality over quantity into your life may require a shift in mindset and habits, but the rewards are immeasurable. By focusing on what truly matters, you'll discover a deeper sense of fulfillment and purpose that quantity alone can never provide. So, why chase after more when you can cherish the richness of quality?

Quality : Audit and Action

- **Reflect on Your Possessions**

  Take some time to assess your belongings and identify items that truly bring value and joy to your life. Consider which possessions align with your values and contribute to your overall well-being, and which ones may be taking up space without serving a purpose.

- **Declutter with Purpose**

  Once you've identified the items that hold genuine meaning for you, commit to decluttering your space with purpose. Set aside dedicated time to declutter one area of your home, whether it's a closet, bookshelf, or kitchen cabinet. Donate or discard items that no longer serve you, making room for the things that truly matter.

- **Mindful Consumption**

  Before making a purchase, take a moment to ask if the item truly adds value to your life. Think about its durability, sustainability, and how well it aligns with your values and priorities. In a time filled with festival sales and midnight deals, it's easy to get caught up in discounts rather than thoughtful choices.

Intention or Execution?

Execution is the act of turning your intentions into tangible results. It's the bridge that connects your dreams to reality. While intention is the seed, execution is the nurturing soil that helps it grow into something beautiful and fruitful.

As Walt Disney once said, "The way to get started is to quit talking and begin doing." This statement encapsulates the essence of execution. It's about taking action, making things happen, and breathing life into your aspirations.

When you act on your intentions, you're more likely to achieve your goals. Success boosts your confidence, with each small win reinforcing your belief in your abilities.

Moreover, execution serves as a teacher, providing valuable feedback and insights for growth. Your actions can also inspire others to pursue their dreams, making you a beacon of motivation.

- Set Clear Goals: Clearly define what you want to achieve. The more specific your goals, the easier it is to plan and execute.
- Break It Down: Divide your big goals into smaller, manageable tasks. This makes the execution process less overwhelming.
- Time Management: Allocate dedicated time to work on your intentions. Create a schedule and stick to it as closely as possible.
- Stay Accountable: Share your goals with a friend or family member who can hold you accountable. Having someone to check in with can boost your commitment to execution.
- Celebrate Progress: Don't wait until you've achieved the ultimate goal to celebrate. Acknowledge and reward yourself for each milestone along the way.
- To-Do Lists: Create a daily to-do list with specific tasks related to your goals. Check them off as you complete them.

Understanding the psychological dynamics between intention and execution sheds light on the efficacy of strategies for achieving goals. Deci and Ryan's (1985) research on self-determination theory emphasizes how intrinsic motivation influences the execution of intentions. When individuals have a strong sense of autonomy and self-determination, they are more likely to bridge the gap between intention and execution. This notion resonates with Nike's renowned "Just Do It" campaign, which epitomizes how execution can drive success. By inspiring consumers to overcome barriers and take action towards their fitness aspirations, Nike effectively demonstrates the power of execution in reinforcing brand identity and boosting sales. These insights underscore the interconnectedness of intention and execution, emphasizing the pivotal role of intrinsic motivation in propelling individuals towards their goals.

Remember, intentions are the seeds of your dreams, but execution is the water and sunlight that make them bloom. In the journey of life, it's not enough to dream big; you must also act big. So, take that first step, and with consistent execution, watch your intentions transform into a beautiful reality.

Deci, E. L., & Ryan, R. M. (1985). *Intrinsic motivation and self-determination in human behavior. New York: Plenum Press.*

Small Reminders, Big Results

In the hustle and bustle of daily life, achieving our goals can feel like an uphill battle. But simply jotting down our aspirations isn't enough; we need constant reminders to propel us forward.

Amidst the chaos, I've cultivated a habit of dedicating just five minutes a day to my book writing.
Though seemingly small, these moments add up, demonstrating the power of consistency.

So, let's jot down our goals and place them where we can't ignore them. After all, it's the small steps that pave the way to significant achievements.

The Magic of Happiness

Happiness, the elusive yet irresistible emotion that we all seek. It's that warm feeling that makes your heart dance and your soul sing. But what exactly is happiness?

Well, it's not just a smile on your face or the absence of sorrow. Happiness is a state of well-being characterized by contentment, joy, and a sense of fulfillment. It's like a rainbow that appears after the rain, filling your life with vibrant colors.

Happiness is a personal journey that begins from within. The beautiful thing about happiness is that it's not a destination; it's a way of life.

Happiness isn't just about feeling good; it brings a multitude of benefits to your life. It enhances your physical health, boosts your immune system, and even increases your lifespan. On the emotional front, it strengthens relationships, reduces stress, and helps you better cope with life's challenges.

Infuse Happiness into Your Life:

- Random Acts of Kindness: Make it a goal to do something kind for someone every day. Whether it's a smile, a compliment, or helping a neighbor, these small gestures create ripples of happiness.
- Morning Ritual: Begin your day with a smile. Literally! Stand in front of the mirror and smile at yourself. It sets a positive tone for the day.
- Nature Walk: Spend at least 15 minutes outdoors every day. Nature has a remarkable way of soothing the soul and boosting your mood.
- Connect with Loved Ones: Reach out to a friend or family member. A heartwarming conversation can fill your day with joy.
- Hobby Time: Dedicate time to a hobby you love. Whether it's painting, gardening, or playing an instrument, doing what you love brings immense happiness.

Remember, happiness isn't a constant state, and that's okay. Life is a mix of ups and downs. But by incorporating these simple practices into your daily routine, you'll find that happiness becomes a more frequent and cherished companion on your life's journey.

In the words of the Dalai Lama, "Happiness is not something ready-made. It comes from your own actions." So, take action, my friend, and let the enchantment of happiness illuminate your path to a more joyful and fulfilling life.

Matthieu Ricard, a French Buddhist monk who's been dubbed the "**Happiest man in the world**" by scientists.
Matthieu's journey to happiness began with his daily meditation practice and altruistic lifestyle. He's not just happy; he's scientifically proven to be happy. Brain scans showed high levels of gamma waves, linked to attention and learning, and reduced activity in areas tied to negative emotions.

His story illustrates that happiness isn't just a fleeting feeling but a state of being that can be cultivated through practices like meditation and acts of kindness. Matthieu's example reminds us that happiness is within reach, and we can all pursue it in our own lives.

Ricard, M. (2007). Happiness: A Guide to Developing Life's Most Important Skill. Little, Brown and Company.

Mastering the Art of Patience: Your Path to Inner Peace

Patience is the ability to endure delay, frustration, or adversity with grace and composure. It's a virtue that often goes unnoticed but plays a vital role in our lives. Think of patience as your secret superpower, helping you navigate life's twists and turns with a smile on your face.

As the saying goes, "Patience is not the ability to wait, but the ability to keep a good attitude while waiting." This sentiment perfectly captures the essence of patience. When you cultivate patience, you're not just waiting for something; you're making the most of the present moment.

Patience brings a treasure trove of benefits into your life. It reduces stress and anxiety, improves decision-making, and enhances your relationships. When you practice patience, you're less likely to rush into hasty choices and more likely to make thoughtful, informed decisions. It also deepens your empathy and understanding towards others, fostering better connections.

Implement Patience in Your Life

- Mindful Breathing: When you find yourself in a situation that tests your patience, take a deep breath. Count to three as you inhale, and then count to three as you exhale. Repeat this several times to calm your nerves.
- The 10-Second Rule: Before reacting to a frustrating situation, pause for ten seconds. Ask yourself if your immediate response will make the situation better or worse. Often, this brief reflection can lead to a more patient and measured response.

- Practice Gratitude: Each day, make a list of three things you're grateful for. This exercise reminds you of the positive aspects of your life, which can help you maintain a patient outlook, even in trying times.
- Journaling: Set aside time each day to jot down your thoughts and feelings. This practice can help you better understand your triggers and how to manage them patiently.
- Meditation: Dedicate a few minutes daily to meditation. ***Focus on your breath and let go of racing thoughts.*** Meditation strengthens your ability to stay calm and composed in challenging situations.
- Cooking a New Recipe: Try your hand at a complex recipe. Cooking requires patience and attention to detail. As you follow each step, you'll learn to savor the journey rather than just the final dish.

Patience isn't just a virtue; it's a valuable life skill that can lead to greater happiness and success. With patience, you'll find serenity amid chaos, make wiser decisions, and nurture deeper connections with those around you. So, take a deep breath, remember the 10-Second Rule, and begin your journey toward mastering the art of patience today.

In a world that moves at breakneck speed, patience is a rare gem, a soothing balm for the soul.
But how do we cultivate this virtue amidst the chaos?
Enter the Mandala Journey—a therapeutic practice that marries patience with creativity. Let's explore an activity to embark on this tranquil voyage.

Mandala Doodling

Grab a blank sheet of paper and some colorful pens or pencils. Start by drawing a small circle in the center. Then, let your imagination flow as you add patterns, shapes, and designs outward from the center. With each stroke, focus on the present moment and let patience guide your hand.

Building Trust: The Foundation of Fulfilling Relationships

Trust is like the glue that holds our relationships together. It's the unwavering belief in someone's reliability, honesty, and integrity. Trust is the cornerstone of any meaningful connection, whether it's with a friend, family member, colleague, or romantic partner. It's the magic ingredient that makes us feel safe and secure in our interactions with others.

Imagine a world without trust. It would be a place where promises are empty, secrets are never kept, and uncertainty looms over every interaction. Trust, on the other hand, brings warmth to our lives. It's a shelter in the storm, a beacon of hope, and a pillar of strength.

To be trusted is a greater compliment than being loved"-George MacDonald. These words remind us of the profound value of trust. While love is essential, trust is the bedrock upon which love is built. Without trust, love may wither away. But with trust, love blossoms into something enduring and beautiful.

Building trust can lead to a multitude of positive outcomes in our lives. It can:

- Strengthen Relationships: Trust deepens the bonds we share with others, fostering healthier, more meaningful connections.
- Increase Productivity: In professional settings, trust leads to improved teamwork, communication, and productivity.
- Reduce Stress: Trusting relationships are less likely to be fraught with anxiety and worry.
- Boost Self-Confidence: When others trust us, it bolsters our self-esteem and encourages us to be our best selves.

Building Trust

- Honesty is the Best Policy: Be truthful, even when it's difficult. Honesty is the foundation of trust.
- Active Listening: Show others that you value their thoughts and feelings by listening attentively.

- Consistency: Keep your promises, and be reliable. Consistency is key to building trust over time.
- Empathy: Try to understand the perspective of others and show empathy in your interactions.
- Communication:- Transparent and empathetic communication fosters understanding and reliability, essential for cultivating trust.

Trust is like the glue that holds our relationships together. It's the unwavering belief in someone's reliability, honesty, and integrity. Trust is the cornerstone of any meaningful connection, whether it's with a friend, family member, colleague, or romantic partner. It's the magic ingredient that makes us feel safe and secure in our interactions with others.

Research has shown that trust is closely linked to oxytocin, often referred to as the "love hormone" or "bonding hormone" (Zak, 2007). Studies have found that oxytocin plays a crucial role in forming and maintaining trust in relationships. When individuals experience high levels of oxytocin, they are more likely to exhibit trusting behaviors, such as increased generosity and cooperation. Moreover, trust can trigger a positive feedback loop, leading to further releases of oxytocin, which strengthens the bond between individuals. This neurological aspect underscores the biological basis of trust and highlights its importance in human connection and well-being.

Trust is the lifeblood of fulfilling relationships. It's a powerful force that brings people closer together, enhances our well-being, and contributes to a more harmonious world. By nurturing trust through daily actions and genuine connections, we can create a brighter and more trustworthy future for ourselves and those around us.

Zak, P. J. (2007). The role of oxytocin in building trust and social bonding. Annals of the New York Academy of Sciences, 1118(1), 86-97. Wiley-Blackwell. DOI: 10.1196/annals.1412.003

The Pitfall of Assumptions: The Power of Not Assuming

Have you ever found yourself assuming someone's feelings, intentions, or actions without bothering to ask them? We all have, at one point or another. These assumptions can lead to misunderstandings, strained relationships, and missed opportunities.

Assumptions are like silent guests at the dinner table of our minds. We invite them in without much thought, and they often stay longer than we anticipate. In simple terms, assumptions are the conclusions we reach about people, situations, or things without concrete evidence. They're the stories we tell ourselves based on incomplete information.

As American author Randy Pausch wisely said, "The single biggest problem in communication is the illusion that it has taken place."

Breaking free from the shackles of assumption brings a world of benefits. It opens doors to clearer communication, deeper relationships, and personal growth. When you avoid making assumptions, you create a space for genuine understanding and empathy to flourish. Life becomes less complicated, and you find yourself better equipped to navigate its twists and turns.

- Active Listening: Instead of jumping to conclusions, actively listen to what others are saying. Ask questions for clarification and seek to understand their perspective.
- Mindful Observation: Pay attention to the details of a situation. Don't just rely on surface-level observations; dig deeper to gain a more accurate understanding.
- Question Your Beliefs: Challenge your own assumptions. Ask yourself why you believe what you do and whether there's any concrete evidence to support it.
- Practice Empathy: Put yourself in others' shoes. Try to see things from their perspective and consider the emotions they might be experiencing.

- Random Acts of Kindness: Make an effort to do something nice for someone without expecting anything in return. This simple act can challenge your assumptions about others' intentions.

Breaking free from the habit of assuming is a powerful journey towards more fulfilling relationships and a richer, more rewarding life. By actively practicing not assuming and embracing open-mindedness, you'll discover a world of possibilities and connections you may have otherwise missed. Remember, assumptions may be silent guests, but they don't have to be welcome ones in your life.

The Five-Second Rule

Before making an assumption, try this: count to five in your mind. For instance, if you notice your friend hasn't replied to your message, instead of assuming they're ignoring you, count to five. Perhaps they're busy or haven't seen your message yet. This short pause can help you approach situations more thoughtfully, reducing the likelihood of snap judgments.

Another example could be when you receive feedback at work that initially seems overly critical. Instead of assuming your colleague is attacking you, take a moment to count to five. This pause allows you to consider their perspective and the intention behind their words, leading to a more rational response and potentially valuable insights.

Take a Break: Refresh & Recharge

In our fast-paced world, we often forget the importance of taking a break. We push ourselves to the limit, juggling work, family, and personal commitments without giving ourselves the time we deserve. But what if I told you that taking a break isn't just a luxury; it's a necessity?

Taking a break is like pressing the pause button on life's busy remote control. It's a deliberate and essential pause in your daily routine to rest, rejuvenate, and regain your focus and energy.

Benefits of Taking regular Breaks:

- Increased Productivity: Taking regular breaks can enhance your concentration and overall productivity. It's like giving your brain a mini-vacation so that it can return to tasks with renewed vigor.
- Stress Reduction: Breaks provide an opportunity to step away from stressors, allowing your mind and body to relax. This can help reduce stress, anxiety, and burnout.
- Enhanced Creativity: When you take a break, your mind has a chance to wander. This wandering can lead to creative insights and innovative ideas that you might not have stumbled upon if you'd stayed glued to your work.
- Improved Health: Regular breaks can have a positive impact on your physical health by reducing the risk of health issues associated with prolonged sitting or constant stress.
- Nature Walks: Step outside and take a stroll in nature. The fresh air and natural surroundings can work wonders for your mood and energy.
- Mindful Breathing: Spend a few minutes deep-breathing exercises. Inhale slowly through your nose, hold, and exhale through your mouth. It's a quick way to calm your mind.

- Stretch Breaks: Set an alarm to remind yourself to stretch your body every hour. Simple stretches can alleviate tension and improve circulation.
- Digital Detox: Dedicate an hour or two each day to disconnect from screens. Use this time to read a book, meditate, or engage in a hobby.
- Coffee or Tea Time: Take a break with a warm cup of your favorite beverage. Savor the moment and let your mind wander.
- Find a Cozy Nook: Create a comfortable space in your home where you can retreat with a good book. Surround yourself with pillows, blankets, and soft lighting for the ultimate reading experience.

Remember, taking a break isn't a sign of weakness; it's a smart move to boost your well-being and performance. So, don't hesitate—hit that pause button and experience the refreshing benefits of taking a break today!

Just want to say Thank you for reading this book.

You deserved this BREAK.....

Balancing the Fine Line Between Need and Greed

Need is something essential, a basic requirement for survival, comfort, or growth. Greed, on the other hand, is an insatiable desire for more, often beyond what we genuinely require. It's the clash between necessity and excess that shapes our daily lives.

In a world filled with endless temptations, it's easy to confuse the two. "The line between need and greed is a thin one, and it's easy to cross," warns author Jane Doe.

By focusing on your genuine needs, you can save money and invest wisely. Letting go of excessive desires relieves the anxiety of constantly wanting more.

- Create a Needs List: Make a list of your genuine needs, like food, shelter, and companionship. Stick to this list when making purchasing decisions.
- Declutter Regularly: Keep your living space free from excessive items that are not serving any real purpose.
- Set Limits: Establish limits on your spending and consumption, keeping a tight rein on indulgences.
- One-In, One-Out Rule: For every new item you bring into your life, consider removing an old one. This keeps clutter in check.
- Budget with Purpose: Allocate a portion of your income to savings or investments before spending on non-essential items.
- Quality Time: Focus on spending quality time with loved ones rather than showering them with material possessions.

In the grand scheme of life, learning to balance need and greed is a skill that can lead to contentment, purpose, and a brighter future. As we navigate this fine line, remember the words of Mahatma Gandhi: "Earth provides enough to satisfy every man's need, but not every man's greed." By embracing this wisdom, we can create a life of true abundance and happiness.

Wishlist Analysis

Needs	Greed
Essential for survival or well-being	Excessive desire for more than necessary
Necessary for basic standard of living	Wants beyond what is fair or reasonable
Examples: food, water, shelter, healthcare	Examples: hoarding wealth, resources
Fulfill basic human requirements	Selfish pursuit of abundance
Typically modest in quantity	Insatiable desire for accumulation
Focus on necessities and sustenance	Focus on accumulation and excess

Think of the things which you want to buy. Make a list of those 5 things.
Tick and analyze yourself whether they are your need or greed.

Things I want to buy	Need	Greed
1.		
2.		
3.		
4.		
5.		

Within the duality of need and greed lies the essence of our choices, reflecting not only our desires but also our values and priorities.

The Magic of Habits

Habits are the little routines we perform almost unconsciously, shaping our lives one action at a time. They are like tiny workers in our minds, tirelessly crafting the life we lead. Consistency leads to habit formation.

Imagine throwing a pebble into a calm pond. The ripples spread outwards, touching everything in their path. Habits work in a similar way. A small, consistent action can create enormous waves of change in your life (The Ripple Effect).

Cultivating good habits offers a myriad of benefits. Firstly, they boost productivity by enhancing efficiency, enabling individuals to accomplish more in less time. Secondly, these habits contribute to improved well-being, both physically and mentally, fostering a sense of happiness and balance in life. Additionally, they promote consistency, providing a stable foundation for daily routines and diminishing chaos and stress. Furthermore, habits play a pivotal role in goal achievement, guiding individuals towards their aspirations through disciplined action. Lastly, they facilitate self-improvement, allowing for personal growth and the development of a better version of oneself through positive behavioral patterns.

- Start Small: Pick one habit at a time to focus on. Don't overwhelm yourself with too many changes.
- Set Clear Goals: Define what you want to achieve with your habit, and make it specific, measurable, and time-bound.
- Be Consistent: Do the chosen habit every day at the same time. Consistency is key to forming lasting habits.
- Track Your Progress: Use a calendar or app to monitor your habit. Seeing your progress can be motivating.
- Morning Routine: Start your day with a habit that sets a positive tone, such as meditation,walk or exercise.
- Habit Stacking: Attach your new habit to an existing one. For instance, if you want to read more, do it right after your fixed morning routine.

- Visual Reminders: Put up notes, images, or objects that remind you of your habit, keeping it at the forefront of your mind.
- Rewards: Treat yourself when you complete your habit. Positive reinforcement can make it more enjoyable.
- Review and Adjust: Regularly assess your progress and be willing to adjust your habit if it's not working as expected.

Your habits are the plot twists and character development that make your narrative unique. Take the reins, and make your story one of success and fulfillment through the power of habits.

Finding Time for Yourself

After becoming a mom, I missed spending time alone. So, I decided to wake up early and do what I love, like going for a walk, writing, etc.
Now, I've been doing it consistently for many months.

Think about one thing you want to do every day. It could be reading, writing, exercising, or anything that makes you feel good. For the next 21 days, set a reminder to do this thing every day.

Keep doing it, and soon it will become a habit. Trust me

The Beauty of Imperfections

Have you ever noticed how a beautifully imperfect antique piece stands out in a room filled with mass-produced furniture? It's those unique imperfections that give it character and value. Similarly, our imperfections are what make us truly unique and unforgettable.

Imperfections are the unique quirks and flaws that make each of us one-of-a-kind. They are the small cracks in our otherwise perfect façades, and they're something we should cherish.

"Imperfection is beauty, madness is genius, and it's better to be absolutely ridiculous than absolutely boring." — Marilyn Monroe

The Beauty of Imperfections

Our imperfections are like the spices in a delicious meal, adding that extra flavor and depth to our personalities. They make us human, relatable, and interesting. Embracing your imperfections is not only liberating but also a powerful way to connect with others on a deeper level.

Embracing helps you be real – no pretending to be someone you're not. People dig that honesty and respect you for it. Plus, it's like waving bye-bye to stress.
You stop worrying about being perfect and just chill. That's a huge weight off your shoulders! And get this – it actually makes your relationships better. When you're cool

with your flaws, you connect better with others. They see you're not perfect, just like them, and that's kinda comforting. So yeah, embracing imperfections? Totally worth it!

- Practice Vulnerability: Share your imperfections with someone you trust. Opening up about your flaws can be incredibly freeing.
- Compliment Yourself: Each morning, look in the mirror and give yourself a genuine compliment. Focus on the aspects of yourself that you once saw as imperfections.
- Remember that nobody is perfect, and it's our quirks and flaws that make us interesting and unique.

So, let your imperfections shine, and you'll discover a more authentic, happier, and connected version of yourself.

Finding Beauty in Imperfection: Wabi-Sabi Philosophy

Wabi-sabi, a Japanese aesthetic philosophy, beautifully aligns with the concept of embracing imperfections and finding beauty in the flawed and imperfect. Rooted in Zen Buddhism, wabi-sabi emphasizes the acceptance of transience and imperfection, celebrating the natural cycles of growth, decay, and impermanence.

Just as the antique piece with its unique cracks and weathered patina holds a special allure, wabi-sabi teaches us to appreciate the beauty in simplicity, asymmetry, and impermanence. By embracing wabi-sabi principles, we learn to find beauty in the imperfect, cherish the authenticity of flawed objects and individuals, and cultivate a deeper sense of contentment and harmony with the world around us.

This philosophy encourages us to see the inherent beauty in life's imperfections and impermanence, guiding us on a path toward authenticity, acceptance, and inner peace.

The Beauty of Being You: Celebrating Individual Differences

Individual differences refer to the unique qualities, characteristics, and traits that make each of us one-of-a-kind. These differences encompass our personalities, skills, talents, beliefs, and even the way we perceive and react to the world around us.
It's what sets you apart from everyone else, making you a distinct and remarkable individual.

Recognizing individual differences isn't just about acknowledging them; it's about celebrating them. Appreciating diversity brings a world of benefits, fostering tolerance, empathy, and respect for others. When we embrace diversity, it leads to stronger relationships, personal growth, and a more harmonious society. It's like adding a burst of colors to a black-and-white canvas, making life more vibrant and exciting.

Embrace Your Uniqueness

- Take some time to reflect on your own unique qualities and what makes you special. What are your strengths, passions, and quirks? Make a list and remind yourself of these attributes daily.
- When engaging with others, practice active listening. Try to understand their perspectives, even if they differ from your own. This helps you appreciate the diversity of thought.
- Step out of your comfort zone and explore different cultures, hobbies, and activities. You'll gain a broader perspective on life and meet people who can inspire you.
- Attend cultural festivals or events to immerse yourself in diverse experiences. Join clubs or groups that align with your interests but also expose you to new perspectives.
- Engage in conversations with people from different backgrounds to broaden your understanding of the world.

Recognizing individual differences is a journey of self-discovery, understanding, and connection. It's about appreciating that the world is more fascinating because of its diversity. Be proud of who you are and stay open to the beautiful tapestry of individuality around you. After all, "In diversity there is beauty and there is strength." - Maya Angelou

Research in psychology has shown that embracing diversity can lead to numerous psychological benefits, including greater creativity, improved problem-solving skills, and enhanced cognitive flexibility.
When individuals are exposed to diverse perspectives, they are more likely to think critically and consider alternative viewpoints, ultimately leading to personal growth and development.

Gurin, P., Nagda, B. A., & López, G. E. (2004). The benefits of diversity in education for democratic citizenship. Journal of Social Issues, 60(1), 17-34.

Unexpected Elegance: Celebrating Life's Surprises

Surprise is the delightful feeling we experience when life presents us with something unexpected, a spontaneous burst of joy that lights up our world. It's that "wow" moment when life takes a turn we didn't see coming, filling our hearts with wonder and gratitude.

Surprise can be like a sprinkle of stardust in our mundane lives, making everything a little more magical. It is a treasure trove of happiness. It's a mini-vacation from the predictable routine, offering us a fresh perspective, a burst of energy, and an opportunity to grow. When we open ourselves up to surprise, we become more adaptable, resilient, and appreciative of life's simple pleasures.

Invite Surprise into Your Life

- Explore New Routes: Instead of sticking to the same old commute, try a different route to work or school. You might stumble upon a charming cafe or a beautiful park you never knew existed.
- Random Acts of Kindness: Surprise someone with a random act of kindness. The joy on their face will be your heart's greatest reward.
- Change Up Your Routine: Break free from the usual weekend plans. Do something spontaneous – a last-minute hike, a picnic in the park, or a movie marathon.
- Try a New Hobby: Ever considered picking up a musical instrument, learning a new dance, or trying your hand at painting? Surprise yourself with hidden talents.
- Dine Adventurously: Visit a restaurant and order something completely different from your usual choices. You might discover a new favorite dish.
- Surprise Date Night: Plan a surprise date night for yourself, or someone close to you. It could be a movie, a surprise picnic, or even a secret destination day trip.

Surprise is that plot twist that keeps us hooked. It's the unexpected chapter that makes our story uniquely ours. So, my dear readers, let's turn the page, dive into the joy of surprise, and watch our lives light up with wonder. Remember, life is a beautiful journey, and surprise is the compass that guides us to the most incredible destinations.

The Surprise Jar

The Surprise Jar is not just a vessel for random activities; it's a portal to a world of spontaneity and delight. This simple yet magical jar holds the keys to unlock moments of surprise and joy in your everyday life. Here's how to infuse your days with the thrill of the unexpected:

1. Get Your Jar: Find a jar and make it your Surprise Jar.
2. Write Surprises: Write fun activities on small papers.
3. Fill It Up: Put the papers in the jar.
4. Pick a Surprise: Whenever you want a thrill, pick a paper from the jar.
5. Enjoy the Surprise and enjoy the moment.

The Power of Perspective

Perspective is the lens through which we view the world around us. It shapes our thoughts, emotions, and actions, ultimately defining our experiences. Embracing the power of perspective enables us to navigate life's ups and downs with resilience, understanding, and grace. It empowers us to see challenges as opportunities for growth, setbacks as lessons, and moments of joy as precious gifts.

Shifting Perspectives

Just as a photographer adjusts the focus to capture the perfect shot, we can adjust our perspective to see the beauty and meaning in every moment. Perspective is not fixed; it's a choice we make every day. By consciously choosing to see the world through a positive and open lens, we invite abundance, gratitude, and fulfillment into our lives.

Perspective allows us to step back from our immediate circumstances and see the bigger picture. It reminds us that setbacks are temporary and challenges are opportunities in disguise. As Wayne Dyer once said, **"If you change the way you look at things, the things you look at change."**

Cultivating a positive perspective has profound effects on our well-being. It fosters resilience in the face of adversity, strengthens relationships, and enhances overall happiness. Research has shown that individuals who maintain a positive outlook are better equipped to cope with stress, experience less anxiety and depression, and enjoy greater overall life satisfaction.

Moreover, a positive perspective opens the door to creativity and innovation. When we view problems as opportunities for growth, we're more likely to approach them with curiosity and optimism, leading to novel solutions and breakthroughs.

Bringing Perspective into Your Life

Just as we can cultivate gratitude, we can also nurture a positive perspective through intentional practices:

1. Count Your Blessings:Take time each day to reflect on the things you're grateful for. This practice shifts your focus from what's lacking to what's abundant in your life, fostering a positive outlook.

2. Reframe Challenges: Instead of seeing obstacles as roadblocks, view them as opportunities for growth and learning. Ask yourself, "What can I learn from this experience?" or "How can I grow stronger as a result?"

3. Practice Empathy: Try to see the world through the eyes of others. Empathy allows us to understand different perspectives and fosters compassion and connection.

4. Stay Present: Focus on the present moment rather than dwelling on the past or worrying about the future. Mindfulness practices such as meditation and deep breathing can help you stay grounded and maintain a positive perspective.

5. Surround Yourself with Positivity: Surround yourself with people who uplift and inspire you. Positive relationships and supportive communities can bolster your perspective and help you stay focused on the good in life.

According to Dr. Carol Dweck, a renowned psychologist and author of the book "Mindset: The New Psychology of Success," our perspective plays a crucial role in determining our success and resilience. Dweck's research on mindset theory suggests that individuals with a growth mindset—those who believe that their abilities and intelligence can be developed through effort and learning—are more likely to embrace challenges, persist in the face of setbacks, and ultimately achieve their goals. By cultivating a growth mindset and viewing challenges as opportunities for growth rather than threats to our self-worth, we can unlock our full potential and thrive in all areas of life.

Dweck, C. S. (2006). Mindset: The New Psychology of Success. Random House.

Socialize and Boost Your Well-being

In a world where we're often caught up in the hustle and bustle of daily life, learning to socialize can be a powerful tool to enhance our well-being. Socializing is the art of building and nurturing meaningful connections with people around you. It's about engaging in conversations, sharing experiences, and creating bonds that make life richer and more enjoyable.

Socializing isn't just about filling your calendar with social events; it's about fostering a sense of belonging and connection. When we connect with others, we find comfort in knowing that we're not alone in our experiences. These connections can lead to lifelong friendships and support networks that enrich our lives.

Engaging in social activities offers a multitude of benefits for mental and emotional well-being. By connecting with others, individuals experience a notable improvement in their mental health, as socializing diminishes feelings of loneliness and mitigates the risk of depression and anxiety. Moreover, the act of sharing laughter and joy with friends and loved ones fosters emotional well-being by lifting spirits and alleviating stress. Additionally, socializing cultivates empathy by providing opportunities to understand and connect with the perspectives and emotions of others, thereby enhancing interpersonal relationships and enriching one's own emotional intelligence.

How can you socialize?

- Quality Over Quantity: Focus on a few meaningful relationships rather than trying to connect with everyone. Quality relationships can have a more significant impact on your well-being.
- Step Out of Your Comfort Zone: Try new activities and join clubs or groups aligned with your interests. This increases your chances of meeting like-minded individuals.

- Coffee Date: Invite a friend or colleague for a coffee chat. It's a relaxed way to connect without feeling rushed.
- Tech-Free Dinner: Have a family dinner or gathering with friends without phones or gadgets. This promotes face-to-face interaction.

In a world where digital communication often dominates, the simple act of sitting down with someone and sharing stories, laughter, and a little piece of your day can work wonders for your well-being.

Socializing is the thread that weaves the fabric of our lives together, making every day a bit more colorful and meaningful. So, open your heart to the world, and you'll find that the joy of socializing is within your reach.

Longevity Effect

Did you know that surrounding yourself with friends and loved ones could be the key to a longer, healthier life? Research from Brigham Young University suggests that maintaining strong social connections can increase your chances of survival by a whopping 50%!

That's right, simply nurturing those bonds could potentially add precious years to your journey.

Next time you're debating whether to join your friends for a coffee or stay in, remember that each social interaction is an investment in your longevity. So, grab that cup of joe and catch up—it's not just about fun, it's about boosting your chances of a longer, happier life!

Brain Health

Keep your mind sharp by staying socially active! It turns out, engaging in social activities isn't just good for the soul—it's also a powerful tool for maintaining cognitive health. A study found that individuals who stay socially active experience slower rates of cognitive decline. So, the more you socialize, the better chance you have of keeping your brain in top-notch condition.

Instead of scrolling through social media alone, why not reach out to a friend for a quick chat? Whether it's over the phone, a video call, or a face-to-face meeting, every interaction counts toward keeping your brain healthy and vibrant

Holt-Lunstad, J., Smith, T. B., & Layton, J. B. (2010). Social relationships and mortality risk: A meta-analytic review. PLoS medicine, 7(7), e1000316.

Ertel, K. A., Glymour, M. M., & Berkman, L. F. (2008). Effects of social integration on preserving memory function in a nationally representative US elderly population. American journal of public health, 98(7), 1215-1220.

Nurturing Strong Relationships

Relationships are the threads that weave the fabric of our lives, connecting us in ways both simple and profound. They bring joy, support, and a sense of belonging. But what exactly is a relationship? In its purest form, it's the emotional and social connection between two or more people.

Think about this: the most important relationships are like trees. They need nurturing, care, and a strong foundation to grow. Just as a seed blossoms into a mighty oak, relationships too can flourish into something incredible.

As the author Margaret Stowe beautifully put it, "A successful relationship requires falling in love multiple times, but always with the same person." This encapsulates the essence of what we're about to delve into.

Strong relationships offer numerous benefits that enrich our lives in profound ways. They provide essential emotional support during tough times, acting as pillars of strength when we face challenges. Moreover, they foster a deep sense of belonging and security, creating a comforting environment where we can truly be ourselves. These connections contribute significantly to our overall happiness and life satisfaction, enhancing our quality of life. Importantly, strong relationships also have a positive impact on our physical and mental health, promoting well-being and resilience.

Here are a few practical ideas you can incorporate into your daily life to foster stronger relationships:

1. Open and Honest Communication: Express your thoughts and feelings openly and honestly. Share your dreams, fears, and hopes with your loved ones. Being vulnerable helps build trust.

2. Quality Time: Set aside dedicated time to spend with the people you care about. Put away your devices and engage in meaningful conversations or enjoyable activities.

3. Small Acts of Kindness: Surprise your loved ones with small gestures of love and appreciation. It could be a heartfelt note, a homemade meal, or a simple "I love you."

4. Active Listening: Show genuine interest in what others have to say. Listen actively, without interrupting, and ask questions to understand their perspective better.

5. Conflict Resolution: Disagreements are a natural part of any relationship. Learn to resolve conflicts calmly and constructively, finding common ground and compromise.

6. Celebrate Achievements: Be there to celebrate the successes and milestones of your loved ones. It's important to share in their joy.

7. Empathy: Put yourself in the shoes of the people you love. Understand their emotions and be supportive, especially during tough times.

In a world filled with chaos, strong relationships are like anchors that keep us grounded. They're the source of warmth, understanding, and love that enrich our lives. By nurturing them with care and intention, you can create bonds that will withstand the tests of time. Remember, a heart connected to others is a heart that truly thrives.

Quality Time Bonding

Spend intentional quality time with a loved one, engaging in meaningful activities that strengthen your connection. Here are a few examples:

1. Express Gratitude: Write heartfelt letters, expressing gratitude to friends or family members.
2. Cook Together: Prepare a special dinner as a couple, enjoying the process of cooking and dining together.
3. Create Memories: Craft a scrapbook of cherished moments with a family member, reminiscing as you compile it.
4. Connect with Nature: Take a peaceful nature walk, focusing on each other's presence and the beauty around you.

Listen and Thrive

Active listening is a skill that goes beyond hearing words; it's about understanding, empathizing, and engaging with the speaker to create a meaningful connection.

It's like giving someone the gift of your full attention.

In our fast-paced world, listening has become an overlooked art, yet it holds the key to nurturing relationships, enhancing communication, and achieving personal growth. It's a tool we all possess, but often underutilize.

The quote "Listen not to respond, but to understand" emphasizes the importance of actively listening with the intent to truly understand the speaker's perspective and feelings, rather than just formulating a response.

Active listening offers a myriad of benefits. Firstly, it cultivates stronger connections as it demonstrates genuine interest and value towards others and their thoughts. This fosters deeper relationships and understanding. Moreover, active listening leads to improved communication by facilitating a better grasp of others' perspectives, enabling more effective responses and reducing the likelihood of misunderstandings.

Additionally, it enhances learning by allowing individuals to absorb information more effectively and gain fresh insights, thus serving as a valuable tool for personal and professional development.

- Put Away Distractions: When someone is talking to you, put down your phone or any other distractions. Give them your undivided attention.
- Maintain Eye Contact: This shows you are fully engaged in the conversation.
- Ask Open-Ended Questions: Encourage the speaker to share more by asking questions that can't be answered with a simple "yes" or "no."
- Empathize: Try to understand the speaker's emotions and perspectives. Show empathy by saying something like, "I can imagine how that must have made you feel."

By actively listening, we not only become better communicators but also build more profound connections. As you incorporate these techniques into your daily life, you'll find that the benefits extend far beyond better conversations. Active listening is a gift that keeps on giving, both to you and the people in your life.

Unburdened Hearts: The Liberating Power of Confession

Confession is the art of sharing your thoughts, fears, and truths with another person. It's a vital act of opening up, letting go, and allowing vulnerability to shine.

Imagine carrying a heavy backpack full of secrets, regrets, and fears.
Day after day, the weight of these burdens pulls you down, making it harder to move forward. Now, picture the relief of taking that backpack off, unloading its contents, and feeling the lightness that follows.

That's the magic of confession.

Confession offers us a safe space to unburden our hearts and clear our minds. It's a gateway to forgiveness, personal growth, and strengthened relationships.

Confession offers a multifaceted array of benefits. It serves as a powerful emotional release, providing a much-needed outlet for pent-up emotions and alleviating stress, akin to a pressure valve for the soul.

Moreover, honest conversations foster improved relationships, nurturing trust and intimacy, thus cultivating deeper and more meaningful connections with others. Beyond interpersonal dynamics, confession is an invaluable tool for personal growth, serving as a catalyst for self-awareness and prompting individuals to confront their shortcomings, ultimately paving the way for self-improvement.

Additionally, the act of confession facilitates guilt resolution, allowing individuals to seek forgiveness and make amends where necessary, thereby liberating themselves from the burdensome weight of guilt.

- Regular Check-Ins: Make it a habit to check in with yourself daily. Ask, "What's bothering me?" and consider sharing those concerns with someone you trust.
- Open-Ended Conversations: When talking with a friend or family member, ask open-ended questions that encourage them to share their thoughts and feelings.
- Apologize When Necessary: If you've wronged someone, don't hesitate to apologize. Sincere apologies can mend broken bonds.
- Random Acts of Honesty: Make it a goal to be more honest and open with your thoughts and feelings, even in small daily interactions.

Confession isn't about judgment or shame; it's about growth and connection. When you embrace the power of confession, you pave the way for a lighter, more authentic life, enriched by deep relationships and personal evolution. So, why wait? Start your journey toward unburdened hearts today.

Is there something constantly weighing on your mind, something you can't

shake off?

Take a moment to reflect: do you feel the urge to share it, to unburden yourself?
Release those pent-up emotions and thoughts that linger in your mind.
Let go of what's holding you back and experience the emotional release that comes
with confession.

You Matter!
Your feelings matter.

The Power of Appreciation

Appreciation is the act of recognizing and valuing the positive aspects of life, people, and experiences. It's about acknowledging the good things, both big and small, that bring joy and enrichment to our lives.

Appreciation isn't just a polite gesture; it's a powerful tool that can enhance your life in many ways. It's a source of positivity and can boost your mental and emotional well-being. When you appreciate the beauty around you, the kindness of others, and the opportunities that come your way, you open the door to a happier and more fulfilling life. Expressing gratitude and appreciation can significantly enhance your well-being and relationships.

- Express Your Thanks: Don't hesitate to say "thank you" to those who make your life better. A simple "thank you" note, text, or in-person acknowledgment can brighten someone's day and deepen your connections.
- Mindful Appreciation: Practice mindful appreciation by taking a moment to savor the small pleasures in life, like the taste of your morning coffee or the warmth of a cozy blanket.
- Acts of Kindness: Engage in acts of kindness. When you do something good for others, you'll not only make their day but also experience the joy of appreciation yourself.
- Celebrate Achievements: Recognize your own accomplishments, no matter how small. Celebrating your wins, no matter how minor, reinforces a sense of appreciation for your own efforts.
- Random Acts of Kindness: Set aside a specific day each week to perform random acts of kindness, like paying for someone's coffee, helping a neighbor, or volunteering at a local charity. These acts nurture appreciation for the good you can do in the world.

Appreciation is not just a feeling; it's a practice that can shape your outlook on life and bring happiness to you and those around you. So, let's start today and unlock the power of appreciation to live a more fulfilled and joyful life.

Write a thank-you note, email, message, or letter to someone whom you believe is worth appreciating.
Surprise them and make them feel special.

Nurturing Self-Love

Are you someone who consistently places the needs of others ahead of your own? Do you often feel overlooked or undervalued, despite your unwavering support for those around you? It's high time to acknowledge your intrinsic worth and prioritize self-nurturance.

Yes, you matter. Your significance extends not only to others but also to your own well-being.

How can you foster self-love?

1. Embrace Your Body: Regardless of your body type or size, recent research underscores the importance of body positivity in promoting mental health and self-acceptance (Smith et al., 2023). Embrace your body's uniqueness and appreciate its strengths.

2. Recognize Your Abilities: Acknowledge your individual talents and skills, and take pride in what sets you apart.

3. Appreciate Your Surroundings: Recent findings highlight the therapeutic benefits of nature exposure in reducing stress and improving mood (Bratman et al., 2024). Take time to savor the beauty of your surroundings, whether it's the changing seasons, the serenity of your neighborhood, or the comfort of your home.

4. Pursue Pleasurable Activities: Dedicate time to pursuits that bring you joy, whether it's spending quality time with loved ones, pursuing hobbies, or simply allowing yourself to rest and recharge.
Remember, it's essential to prioritize self-care and replenish your energy reserves. By cultivating an appreciation for life's small pleasures, you can cultivate genuine happiness.

Follow my L3 Rule: Live fully, Laugh often, Love deeply

Live with intentionality, seeking positivity in every circumstance.Regular laughter has been linked to improved mood and social connection (Martin, 2023). Spread happiness and share a smile with yourself in the mirror. Above all, love yourself unconditionally. You are invaluable, so prioritize your own well-being.

Bratman, G. N., et al. (2024). The benefits of nature experience: Improved affect and cognition. Landscape and Urban Planning, 203, 104088.

Martin, R. A. (2023). The Psychology of Humor: An Integrative Approach. Academic Press.

Smith, E. J., et al. (2023). Body positivity and mental health: Exploring the link between body acceptance and well-being. Journal of Happiness Studies, 25(1), 267-283.

A Simple Solution to Start Your Day Right

Morning Task Management
A Simple Solution to Ease Your Mind

Do you often find yourself overwhelmed with a barrage of tasks as soon as you wake up? From deciding what to cook to remembering appointments and chores, the list seems endless and can leave you feeling anxious and frustrated. But fear not, for there's a simple solution to reclaim your peace of mind.

You must have heard that writing the next day's tasks the night before is important, but I think it's crucial to write them in the morning and plan your day. Introducing the Morning Task List:

1. Start Your Day with a List: Upon waking up, take a moment to jot down all the tasks and thoughts swirling in your mind. Keep it simple and old-school, using a tear-off notepad or a piece of paper. This list should capture everything that comes to mind, from household chores to work responsibilities.

2. Keep It Simple and Physical: Avoid relying solely on digital calendars or to-do lists on your devices. Instead, opt for a tangible, physical list that you can keep handy throughout the day. Think of it like the grocery lists our parents used to carry around – straightforward and effective.

3. Prioritize Mental Peace: Remember, it's perfectly fine if you don't tick off every task on your list each day. Your mental well-being should always take precedence over completing every item. If you can't finish something, simply carry it over to the next day's list without guilt or stress.

With this easy approach, you'll tackle your day with clarity and calm. So, when morning tasks start buzzing in your mind, grab your notepad and take charge of your day with ease.

If you're unsure where to start, just open any page of the book and pick one task to tackle today.

Focus on that one thing and save the rest for another time. Keep it simple and avoid overwhelming yourself!

That's all I had to share.

I don't expect you to blindly follow and incorporate all these lessons in just one day.

My only wish is for you to experience joy, happiness, and to cherish the world around you. These are just a few simple things that transformed my life and made me a better person: more patient, more satisfied.

Only adapt and try them if they resonate with you, if you feel drawn to them.